#A11yBook
A11yBook.com

Making Online Learning Accessible

A Making Work Accessible Handbook

Britne Jenke, CPACC, CPTD, SPHR

Inclusive Pixelation
Las Vegas, NV

Making Online Learning Accessible
A Making Work Accessible Handbook
Second Edition

Reference

Education & Teaching › Higher & Continuing Education › Distance, Open & Online Education

Computers & Technology › Tech Culture & Computer Literacy › Electronic Publishing

Education & Teaching › Teacher Resources › Special Education › General

ISBN

979-8-9896817-2-3 (Paperback)
979-8-9896817-3-0 (Kindle eBook)

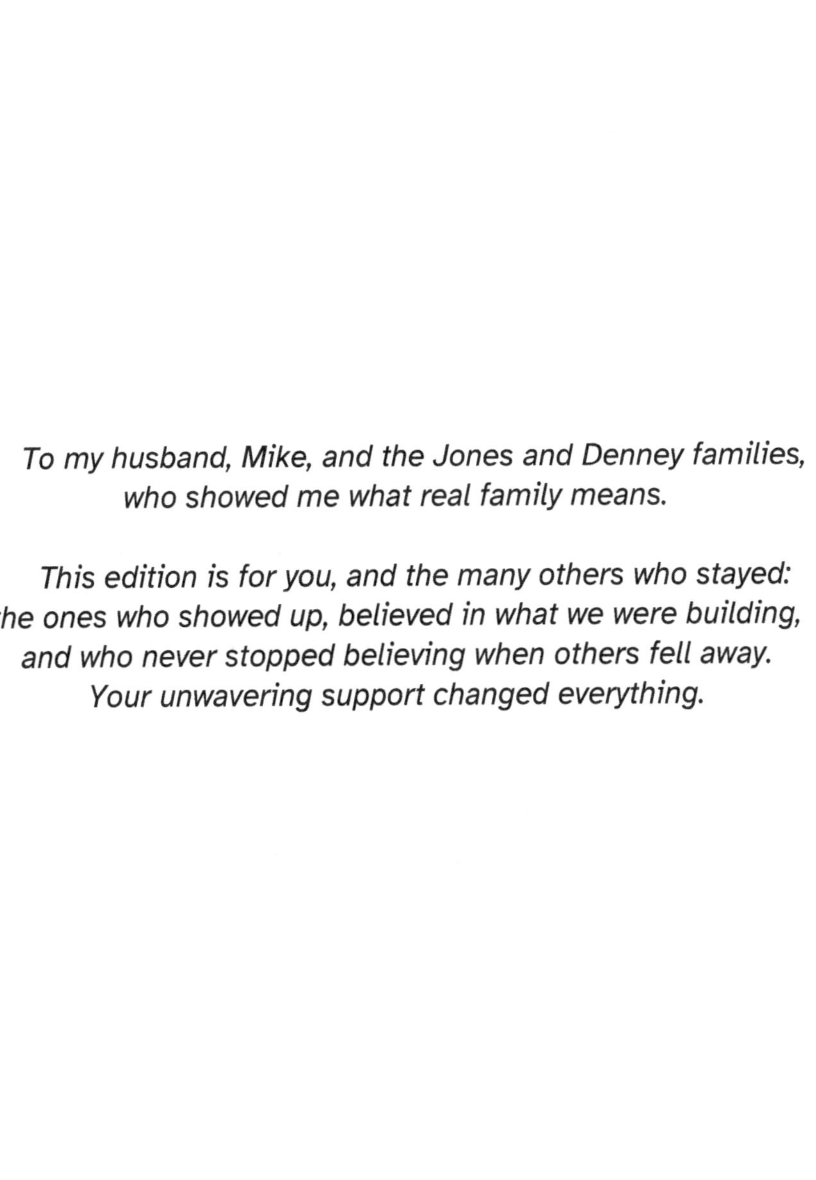

To my husband, Mike, and the Jones and Denney families,
who showed me what real family means.

This edition is for you, and the many others who stayed:
the ones who showed up, believed in what we were building,
and who never stopped believing when others fell away.
Your unwavering support changed everything.

Contents

Second Edition Preface 1

Introduction 2

How to Use This Book 3

Chapter 1: Asynchronous Learning 4

Asynchronous Learning 5

Navigation and Structure 6

- Checklist: Platform Navigation and Structure 13

Color and Font 15

- Checklist: Platform Color and Font 21

Social Interactions 23

- Checklist: Social Interactions 27

Chapter 2: Synchronous Learning 28

Virtual Classrooms, Video Conferencing, and Live Webinars 29

- Checklist: Video Conferencing and Webinars 34

Chapter 3: Multimedia (Audio/Visual) 35

Podcasts and Audio Recordings 36

- Checklist: Podcasts and Audio 40

Recorded Webinars and Video Recordings 41

- Checklist: Recorded Video 45

Images 46

- Checklist: Images 49

Chapter 4: eLearning Modules 50

Navigation and Structure 51

Checklist: eLearning Navigation and Structure 58
Color and Font 60
Checklist: eLearning Color and Font 66
Readability 68
Checklist: eLearning Readability 73
Interactive Elements 74
Checklist: eLearning Interactions 83
Chapter 5: Digital Reference Material 85
Digital Reference 86
Adobe PDF (Portable Document Format) 87
Microsoft Word / PowerPoint 89
Checklist: Specific Document Types 92
Navigation and Structure 93
Checklist: Document Navigation and Structure 97
Color and Font 98
Checklist: Document Color and Font 103
Readability 105
Checklist: Document Readability 110
Appendix 111
References 112
WCAG & ATAG 112
Additional Guidelines 112
Choosing Authoring Tools and Platforms with Accessibility Features 114
VPATs & ACRs 114

Recommended Authoring Tools and Platforms....................115
LMS Accessibility....................115
eLearning Content Creation....................115
Live Training & Audience Participation....................115
Accessible Documents....................116
A Note on Overlays....................116
Accessibility Tools....................117
Reading List....................118
Acknowledgements....................119
About the Author....................120

Second Edition Preface

A lot can happen in two years. Since the first edition of *Making Online Learning Accessible* was released in early 2024, the digital landscape has continued to shift, and our understanding of inclusive design has deepened alongside it.

In this second edition, I have focused on three major areas of improvement:

- **Refreshed Standards**: While WCAG 2.2 remains the bedrock, I have integrated emerging best practices that anticipate the shift toward WCAG 3.0 and the growing importance of other guidelines, such as the Authoring Tool Accessibility Guidelines (ATAG) 2.0.
- **Updated Resources & Tools**: The digital accessibility toolkit is constantly evolving. I have audited every URL and testing tool in the Appendix to ensure you are using the most efficient and accurate resources available today, and have added many new resources to support your work.
- **Expanded Perspectives**: This edition draws new inspiration from recent publications and style guides and the latest UDL (Universal Design for Learning) 3.0 updates. You will find a more robust reading list that includes voices that have pushed the conversation of inclusion forward since our original printing.

Accessibility is not simply a destination. I believe it is a commitment to continuous improvement. Thank you for following this journey with me.

Introduction

Welcome to **Making Online Learning Accessible**! This book is the first in a series of handbooks for practitioners who are looking to take action to make their workplaces more accessible.

This *probably* shouldn't be the first book you pick up about accessibility. I won't spend a lot of time trying to convince you that we should all practice accessibility at work. This book will assume you know the importance of inclusion and making work accessible, and will get right to the practical advice to ensure that it happens.

If you're looking for an introduction to accessibility, please see the reading list in the appendix. Otherwise, I hope you'll use this handbook to jump in and start making your online learning accessible today.

How to Use This Book

Just the Page(s) You Need

This book is designed to be your companion for any online learning you are creating - just identify the chapter and section that applies to your content. Due to this design, some content will be repeated across sections.

Minimum, Recommended, Advanced

Within each topic, the accessibility principles are broken down into minimum, recommended, and advanced suggestions, giving friendlier names to WCAG 2.2 Levels A-AAA. Other accessible design suggestions and best practices from government agencies, researchers, and other publications are also included.

Do the "Minimum" things to ensure basic accessibility. Do the "Recommended" and "Advanced" options to make your online learning even more accessible. This book will also briefly cover the kinds of disabilities you can accommodate thanks to these recommendations and practices.

Checklists, Of Course!

At the end of each section, you will find a short checklist summarizing the recommendations. Use these to get started right away!

For an accessible, downloadable version of each chapter's checklist, visit our online toolbox at **www.A11yBook.com**.

Chapter 1: Asynchronous Learning

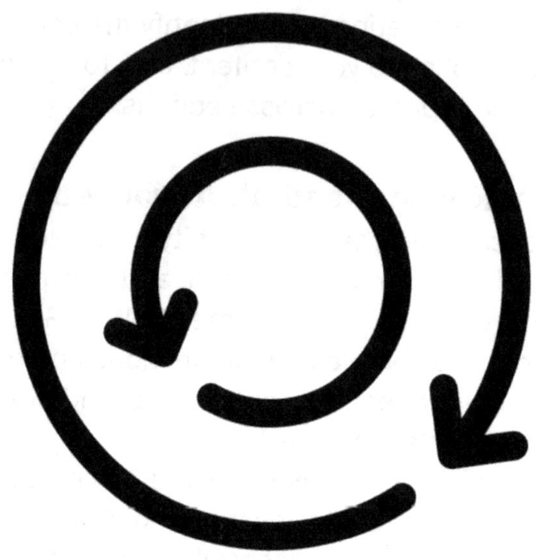

Navigation and Structure
Color and Font
Social Interactions

Asynchronous Learning

What is an asynchronous learning platform? For the purposes of this book, asynchronous learning platforms are defined as any learning platform where your learners log in to complete their activities independent from the instructor and other learners. In practice, they include platforms like Canvas, Nomadic, Moodle, and many others. Note that this section does not fully apply to platforms that function only as a Learning Management System (LMS) for the distribution of course materials.

This chapter will help you make your overall platform accessible through structure and navigation elements, colors and fonts, and social interactions.

Some of these navigation and structural elements may be defined by your software provider, depending on the level of control you have over your content platform. The best practice is to ask about these accessibility requirements when procuring software, and to test the accessibility functionality for yourself.

Navigation and Structure

What Do I Do?

Minimum

Ensure accessible materials and technologies to allow all learners to acquire the same information in an equally effective and usable way.

UDL Guideline 4.2: Optimize access to accessible materials and assistive and accessible technologies and tools

Identify the language used in the platform or page so that assistive technology can read, display, and pronounce the language correctly.

WCAG 2.2 – 3.1.1 Language of Page

All pages should have descriptive titles that make the topic or purpose of the page clear.

WCAG 2.2 - 2.4.2 Page Titled

Use headings and labels to provide clarity around how content is related. For example, an asterisk and red text indicate form fields that are required.

WCAG 2.2 - 1.3.1 Info and Relationships
WCAG 3.0 – 2.7.4 Structure

It should be clear where links will take the learner next, either from the link text itself or the context in the sentence leading up to the link.

WCAG 2.2 – 2.4.4 Link Purpose (In Context)

Make sure the visual presentation of the content matches what's read out by a screen reader by sequencing information correctly. If there are important alerts that appear elsewhere on the page (a cookie statement at the bottom of the page, for example, or anything else the learner must agree to before continuing), make sure they are sequenced to appear at the appropriate time to a screen reader.

WCAG 2.2 - 1.3.2 Meaningful Sequence

Make sure navigation sequences are presented in the correct order by applying a focus order that preserves both meaning and operability.

WCAG 2.2 - 2.4.3 Focus Order

Create a way to bypass blocks of content that are repeated across multiple pages.

WCAG 2.2 - 2.4.1 Bypass Blocks

Make sure all content functionality is operable by the keyboard only. This does not forbid using the mouse or other input methods, but they should be in addition to keyboard functionality.

WCAG 2.2 - 2.1.1 Keyboard
WCAG 3.0 – 2.4.1 Keyboard Interface Input

If the keyboard focus can be moved to content on the page using the keyboard interface, learners should also be able to move focus away from that content also using only the keyboard. If there is a non-standard exit method to remove focus from the content, the learner should be advised of this in advance. This is known commonly as a “keyboard trap,” as it would “trap” a screen reader in a position it cannot get out of.

WCAG 2.2 - 2.1.2 No Keyboard Trap

WCAG 3.0 – 2.4.1 Keyboard Interface Input

WCAG 3.0 – 2.4.2 Physical or Cognitive Effort When Using Keyboard

Provide instructions for understanding and operating content that do not rely solely on sensory characteristics of components (such as shape, color, size, visual location, orientation, or sound).

WCAG 2.2 - 1.3.3 Sensory Characteristics

For any user interface components with labels that include text (such as text entry boxes), the name of the component should contain the same text that is represented visually.

WCAG 2.2 – 2.5.3 Label in Name

If your platform has a help mechanism (including contact details or forms, FAQ pages, or automated systems), it should appear in the same place and in the same order on each page of content.

WCAG 2.2 – 3.2.6 Consistent Help

Recommended

Allow the learner to customize their visual layouts.

UDL Guideline 1.1: Support opportunities to customize the display of information

Provide multiple means of navigation and interaction with learning, including alternative input methods.
UDL Guideline 4.1: Vary and honor the methods for response, navigation, and movement

Give your learners multiple ways to navigate content or to locate a page, except for when content or pages must be followed in a locked sequence or are a step in a process.
WCAG 2.2 - 2.4.5 Multiple Ways

Navigation mechanisms (like a home or back button) that are repeated across multiple pages should appear in the same place and order each time.
WCAG 2.2 - 3.2.3 Consistent Navigation

Components that have the same functionality (like a submit button or search bar) are consistently identified.
WCAG 2.2 - 3.2.4 Consistent Identification

Use headings and labels that describe the topic or purpose of the section or page.
WCAG 2.2 - 2.4.6 Headings and Labels
WCAG 3.0 - 2.7.4 Structure

Identify the language used in each passage or phrase so that assistive technology can read, display, and pronounce the language correctly. Some exceptions include proper names and technical terms.
WCAG 2.2 - 3.1.2 Language of Parts

Do not restrict content views to a single display orientation, such as portrait or landscape, unless the

orientation is essential to the meaning of the content.
WCAG 2.2 - 1.3.4 Orientation

Present content without loss of information or functionality by avoiding scrolling in two dimensions. The best practice is to avoid scrolling within a width of 320 pixels and a height of 256 pixels.
WCAG 2.2 - 1.4.10 Reflow

Visible focus styling should indicate which element the learner is currently focused on.
WCAG 2.2 – 2.4.7 Focus Visible

If a mouse hover or keyboard focus reveals additional content, the content should be persistent until dismissed by the learner.
WCAG 2.2 - 1.4.13 Content on Hover or Focus
WCAG 3.0 – 2.3.1 Keyboard Focus Appearance
WCAG 3.0 – 2.4.2 Physical or Cognitive Effort When Using Keyboard

Status messages are programmed as such so that they may be presented to users of assistive technologies without receiving focus.
WCAG 2.2 – 4.1.3 Status Messages

<u>Advanced</u>

Use section headings to further organize content.
WCAG 2.2 – 2.4.10 Section Headings
WCAG 3.0 – 2.7.4 Structure

Text-based instructions are provided so that intended actions are clear.
WCAG 2.2 - 3.3.5 Help

The purpose of links is clear from the link text alone. Avoid using phrases like "Read More" or "Click Here."
WCAG 2.2 - 2.4.9 Link Purpose (Link Only)
EAPM Style & Accessibility Guide
Accessible Social

Information about the learner's location within the platform is available and persistent.
WCAG 2.2 - 2.4.8 Location

A glossary or other mechanism exists to define unusual words, expand abbreviations, and assist with pronunciation if needed to understand context.
WCAG 2.2 - 3.1.3 Unusual Words
WCAG 2.2 - 3.1.4 Abbreviations
WCAG 2.2 - 3.1.6 Pronunciations
WCAG 3.0 - 2.2.3 Clear Language
UDL Guideline 2.1: Clarify vocabulary, symbols, and language structures
UDL Guideline 6.3: Organize information and resources

Who Benefits?

Users with assistive technology benefit from a range of easy to implement site changes. Clear and consistent page structure with logical headings, descriptive links, and keyboard navigation options enable these learners to understand the content and move around the platform efficiently.

Keyboard shortcuts, intuitive menu design, and other adjustments allow learners with limited dexterity to interact with the platform without relying solely on a mouse.

Simple, organized layouts and predictable navigation patterns support learners with cognitive disabilities in processing information and completing tasks.

Checklist: Platform Navigation and Structure

Minimum

- ❑ Platform and materials are accessible to assistive tech
- ❑ Platform/page language is identified
- ❑ Pages have clear, descriptive titles
- ❑ Headings and labels indicate related content
- ❑ Links clearly indicate where they go
- ❑ Content is sequenced to show alerts in order
- ❑ Focus order reflects navigation order
- ❑ Repeated text can be bypassed
- ❑ All content can be used with the keyboard only
- ❑ NO KEYBOARD TRAPS!
- ❑ Instructions for operation do not rely on senses
- ❑ UI components with text have matching labels
- ❑ FAQ and help pages appear in the same place

Recommended

- ❑ Layout is customizable by the learner
- ❑ Provide multiple ways to interact
- ❑ Allow multiple ways to navigate
- ❑ Navigation elements appear consistently
- ❑ Components with functionality are consistent
- ❑ Headings and labels describe topics and purpose
- ❑ Passage/phrase language(s) are identified
- ❑ Display orientation is not restricted
- ❑ Content display doesn't scroll
- ❑ Focus is visibly styled
- ❑ Additional content on hover is persistent
- ❑ Status messages are presented without focus

Advanced

- ❑ Content is further organized with section headings
- ❑ Instructions are provided as text only
- ❑ Link purpose is clear from link text alone
- ❑ Location information is persistent
- ❑ Glossary is available for definitions and pronunciation

Color and Font

What Do I Do?

Minimum

Provide instructions for understanding and operating content that do not rely solely on sensory characteristics of components (such as shape, color, size, visual location, orientation, or sound).

WCAG 2.2 - 1.3.3 Sensory Characteristics

Do not use color as the only visual means of conveying information, indicating an action, prompting a response, or distinguishing a visual element. Use icons, text, and other formatting to supplement color.

WCAG 2.2 - 1.4.1 Use of Color

Recommended

Allow the learner to customize their text size, contrast, colors, and fonts.

UDL Guideline 1.1: Support opportunities to customize the display of information

Choose dark colored text on a light colored (not white) background, when possible, for improved readability.

The Dyslexia-Friendly Style Guide

Use single color backgrounds, avoiding patterns or pictures which can distract from important context.

The Dyslexia-Friendly Style Guide

Use a contrast ratio of at least 4.5:1 for visual presentation of text and images of text. When the text is large-scale, use a contrast ratio of at least 3:1.

WCAG 2.2 - 1.4.3 Contrast (Minimum)

For graphical objects and interface components, use a contrast ratio of at least 3:1 against adjacent colors.

WCAG 2.2 - 1.4.11 Non-text Contrast

When setting your font styles, do the following:

- Use sans-serif fonts such as Arial, Verdana, and Open Sans so that text appears less crowded.
- Font size should be no smaller than 12pt.
- Headings should be at least 20% larger than surrounding text and are often presented **bold**.

The Dyslexia-Friendly Style Guide
WCAG 3.0 – 2.2.1 Text Appearance

Use **bold** text for emphasis instead of *italics* or underlining, which can make text appear crowded.

The Dyslexia-Friendly Style Guide

Avoid using ALL CAPITAL LETTERS, especially in titles, as this can be more difficult for learners to read than Sentence Case.

The Dyslexia-Friendly Style Guide
Accessible Social
WCAG 3.0 – 2.2.1 Text Appearance

When setting your text and paragraph styles, do the following:

- Line height is at least 1.5 times the font size.

- Paragraph spacing is at least 2 times the font size.
- Letter spacing is at least 0.12 times the font size.
- Word spacing is at least 0.16 times the font size.
- Word spacing is at least 3.5 times letter spacing.

WCAG 2.2 - 1.4.12 Text Spacing
WCAG 3.0 – 2.2.1 Text Appearance
The Dyslexia-Friendly Style Guide

Allow text to be resized without assistive technology - up to 200% without loss of content or functionality. Exceptions are captions and images of text.
WCAG 2.2 - 1.4.4 Resize Text

Avoid use of images of text, unless the image can be customized to the learner's needs or is essential to the meaning of the image, like text in a brand's logo.
WCAG 2.2 - 1.4.5 Images of Text

Avoid "fancy font" generators and other tools that replace text with Unicode symbols. These are either translated into different languages, read unintelligibly, or skipped entirely by screen readers.
Accessible Social

Advanced

Use images of text only for decoration or when an image of text is essential, such as with a brand's logo.
WCAG 2.2 - 1.4.9 Images of Text (No Exception)

Use a contrast ratio of at least 7:1 for visual presentation of text and images of text. When the text is large-scale, use a contrast ratio of at least 4.5:1.

WCAG 2.2 - 1.4.6 Contrast (Enhanced)

When a focus indicator is visible, it has a contrast ratio of at least 3:1 between focused and unfocused states, and is outlined at least 2px thick.

WCAG 2.2 – 2.4.13 Focus Appearance

When presenting blocks of text visually, ensure the following:

- The width of the block is no more than 80 characters (or 40 if logographic characters, such as Japanese or Hieroglyphics).
- Avoid multiple columns of text.
- Text is aligned to the left, right, or center - not justified (aligned to both the left and right, creating uneven spaces between words). Left alignment is preferred, unless the reading direction of the language differs.
- Line spacing is at least 1.5 within paragraphs, and paragraph spacing is 1.5 times larger than line spacing.
- Text can be resized without assistive technology - up to 200% without loss of content or functionality - and without requiring the learner to scroll horizontally on a full-screen window.
- Foreground and background colors can be selected by the learner.

WCAG 2.2 - 1.4.8 Visual Presentation
WCAG 3.0 – 2.2.1 Text Appearance
The Dyslexia-Friendly Style Guide

Avoid using *italic*, underlined, or **bold** text to convey emphasis, as these are not able to be read by screen readers. Instead, convey the emphasis through text. (She emphasized the document was available to anyone.)
EAPM Style & Accessibility Guide
WCAG 3.0 – 2.2.1 Text Appearance

Who Benefits?

Adjustments to colors and fonts primarily benefit learners with vision impairments, however there is also a great benefit for learners with other cognitive limitations. High contrast between text and background is crucial for learners with low vision or color blindness. Simple color palettes and consistent font styles throughout the platform reduce cognitive overload for people with learning disabilities or attention difficulties. Adequate space between lines and paragraphs improves readability, especially for learners with dyslexia or visual processing difficulties.

Checklist: Platform Color and Font

Minimum

- ❑ Instructions for operation do not rely on senses
- ❑ Color is not the only way information is presented

Recommended

- ❑ Learner can customize color and font settings
- ❑ Use light backgrounds with dark text
- ❑ Use single color background (not patterns)
- ❑ Text contrast is 4.5:1 for standard, 3:1 for large text
- ❑ UI components have 3:1 contrast to nearby objects
- ❑ Use a sans-serif font of at least 12pt
- ❑ Headings are at least 20% larger than nearby text
- ❑ **Bold** is used for emphasis instead of underline or *italic*
- ❑ Use Sentence Case NOT ALL CAPS
- ❑ Text line height is at 1.5
- ❑ Spacing after paragraphs is at 2.0
- ❑ Letter spacing is at least 0.12 times the font size
- ❑ Word spacing is at least 0.16 times the font size and 3.5 times the letter spacing
- ❑ Text can be resized without assistive technology
- ❑ Avoid images of text unless customizable or essential
- ❑ Avoid “fancy fonts”

Advanced

- ❑ Use images of text only for decoration
- ❑ Text contrast is 7:1 for standard, 4.5:1 for large text
- ❑ Focus indicator is 2px outline and 3:1 contrast
- ❑ Text blocks are no more than 80 characters wide
- ❑ Text does not appear in columns

- ❑ Text is primarily left aligned
- ❑ Paragraph spacing is at least 1.5 times line spacing
- ❑ Text can be resized without requiring scrolling
- ❑ Learner can select foreground and background colors
- ❑ Avoid using formatting to emphasize text

Social Interactions

What Do I Do?

Minimum

Avoid obscuring links. It should be clear where links will take the learner next, either from the link text itself or the context in the sentence leading up to the link.

WCAG 2.2 - 2.4.4 Link Purpose (In Context)

If a content warning is necessary for sensitive topics, it should be placed at the beginning of the content.

EAPM Style & Accessibility Guide

Recommended

Use inclusive language and avoid discriminatory language and symbols, with consideration to how learners in other cultures may perceive these.

UDL Guideline 2.4: Address biases in the use of language and symbols

Allow for multiple and varied ways of participating and demonstrating understanding.

UDL Guideline 5.4: Address biases related to modes of expression and communication

Create an accepting and supportive social climate with varied sensory stimulation and social demands.

UDL Guideline 7.4: Address biases, threats, and distractions

Create mechanisms for cooperative learning, such as group work, discussion, and peer tutoring, with clear expectations for learner participation.

UDL Guideline 8.3: Foster collaboration, interdependence, and collective learning

Provide models, checklists, and feedback for managing and directing emotional responses, such as frustration or topic phobias.

UDL Guideline 9.2: Develop awareness of self and others
UDL Guideline 9.3: Promote individual and collective reflection

Use #PascalCase (which start each word in the hashtag with a capital letter) or #camelCase (first letter lowercase, other words capitalized) hashtags, making them easier to read, understand, and pronounce by screen readers.

Federal Social Media Toolkit
EAPM Style & Accessibility Guide
Accessible Social

Consider your emoji use:

- Don't replace important words with emoji.
- Don't use emoji as bullet points.
- Place emoji at the end of sentences.

Emoji Accessibility for the Visually Impaired
Accessible Social

Spell out the first use of an acronym or abbreviation, adding the acronym in parenthesis after. This allows learners to associate the sound and spelling of the acronym with the full text.

Federal Accessibility Toolkit

Avoid using capital letters for emphasis, whether in ALL CAPS (yelling) or AlTeRnAtInG cAsE (sarcasm, memes), as these can be improperly interpreted by assistive technology.

Accessible Social
WCAG 3.0 – 2.2.1 Text Appearance

Advanced

Allow for hidden text/spoiler functions that are revealed at the learner's choice for sensitive content. This is a best practice with topics that may require a trigger warning. However, be cautious of how these sections are formatted so they display correctly for screen readers.

Who Benefits?

Building inclusive online spaces means making interactions accessible for everyone, regardless of individual differences. Users of assistive technology benefit from accessible social media through the proper use of hashtags and emojis. Learners with cognitive impairments will benefit from an environment with clear, supportive feedback. By embracing accessibility, social platforms and tools can unlock their full potential as powerful means of connection, communication, and empowerment for everyone.

Checklist: Social Interactions

Minimum

- ❑ Links are not obscured
- ❑ Any content warnings appear before content

Recommended

- ❑ Language and symbols are inclusive
- ❑ Multiple and varied ways to participate
- ❑ Sensory stimulation and social demands are varied
- ❑ Mechanisms exist for cooperative learning
- ❑ Feedback is provided for emotional responses
- ❑ Hashtags are #PascalCase or #camelCase
- ❑ Emojis don't replace important words
- ❑ Emojis are not used as bullets and appear at the end of sentences
- ❑ Acronyms and abbreviations are first spelled out
- ❑ Avoid capital letters for emphasis

Advanced

- ❑ Spoiler text obscures sensitive content

Chapter 2: Synchronous Learning

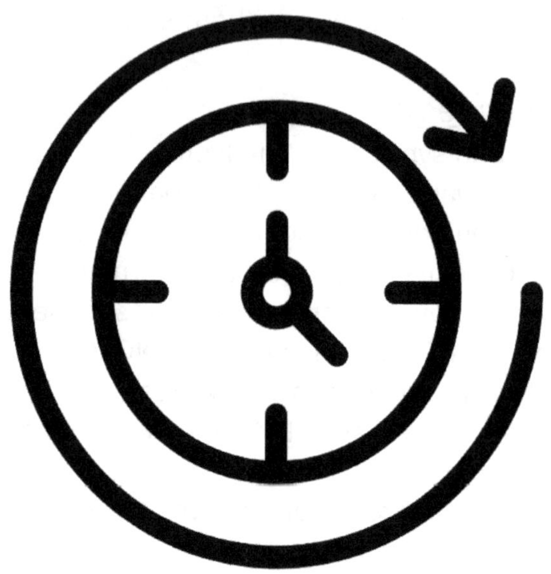

Virtual Classrooms,
Video Conferencing Platforms,
and Live Webinars

Virtual Classrooms, Video Conferencing, and Live Webinars

Virtual classrooms, video conferencing platforms, and webinars are all synchronous learning. At the broadest level, they all do the same thing: instructors and learners are gathered in the same place at the same time.

So, what's the difference? Virtual classrooms have traditionally been more feature-rich than video conferencing platforms, but the gap has narrowed significantly as video conference software is becoming more robust. While virtual classrooms have long included features like interactive whiteboards and breakout rooms, more video conferencing platforms now include these features.

A live webinar is different from a video conference or virtual classroom in how the participants and host(s) interact. A webinar is usually presented continually by the host(s), often with a mechanism to collect questions from the audience to be answered at a designated time. They are often less interactive for participants, compared to a virtual classroom or video conference.

What Do I Do?

Minimum

Ensure accessible materials and technologies to allow all learners to acquire the same information in an equally effective and usable way.

UDL Guideline 4.2: Optimize access to accessible materials and assistive and accessible technologies and tools

Provide instructions for understanding and operating content that do not rely solely on sensory characteristics of components (such as shape, color, size, visual location, orientation, or sound).

WCAG 2.2 - 1.3.3 Sensory Characteristics

Make sure that player controls are usable with a keyboard or keyboard interface.

WCAG 2.2 - 2.1.1 Keyboard

Make sure that learners who navigate using a keyboard or keyboard interface can move focus away from all player controls. Also make sure this can be achieved using standard keyboard keys such as the 'Tab' or 'Arrow' keys, or that learners are made aware if they need to use non-standard keys.

WCAG 2.2 - 2.1.2 No Keyboard Trap
WCAG 3.0 – 2.4.1 Keyboard Interface Input

Recommended

Provide live captions for all audio content.

WCAG 2.2 - 1.2.4 Captions (Live)

WCAG 3.0 – 2.1.4 Captions

Do not restrict content views to a single display orientation, such as portrait or landscape, unless the orientation is essential to the meaning of the content.

WCAG 2.2 - 1.3.4 Orientation

Provide key information in a non-visual alternative, such as spoken descriptions or other auditory cues.

UDL Guideline 1.2: Support multiple ways to perceive information

Provide key information in a non-audio alternative, such as text transcripts or sign languages.

UDL Guideline 1.2: Support multiple ways to perceive information

Present key concepts in one medium with an alternative form available to aid comprehension.

UDL Guideline 2.5: Illustrate through multiple media

UDL Guideline 3.3: Cultivate multiple ways of knowing and making meaning

Allow for multiple and varied ways of participating and demonstrating understanding.

UDL Guideline 5.4: Address biases related to modes of expression and communication

Create an accepting and supportive social climate with varied sensory stimulation and social demands.

UDL Guideline 7.4: Address biases, threats, and distractions

Create mechanisms for cooperative learning, such as group work, discussion, and peer tutoring, with clear expectations for learner participation.

UDL Guideline 8.3: Foster collaboration, interdependence, and collective learning

<u>Advanced</u>

Provide alternatives such as prepared scripts for all time-based audio content.

WCAG 2.2 - 1.2.9 Audio Only (Live)

Provide alternatives for all prerecorded media content.

WCAG 2.2 - 1.2.8 Media Alternative (Prerecorded)

Provide sign language interpretation for all prerecorded audio content. Consider live sign language interpretation as needed.

WCAG 2.2 - 1.2.6 Sign Language (Prerecorded)

Who Benefits?

Learners with auditory disabilities (such as deafness, hard-of-hearing/hearing loss, or auditory processing disorders) will face challenges with synchronous learning content that contains audio. Some learners may use assistive technology, such as hearing aids or personal listening devices, to access synchronous learning content.

Learners with cognitive impairments (learning and intellectual disabilities, for example) or neurodiversity (ADHD, autism spectrum, etc.) may also benefit from making synchronous learning content accessible. For example, those with sensory disabilities (such as blindness or deafness) and learning disabilities (such as dyslexia) may all require different ways of approaching content.

Some learners may grasp information quicker or more efficiently through visual or auditory means compared to printed text. Also, learning and transfer of learning occur when multiple representations are used, because these allow learners to make connections within, as well as between, concepts.

Checklist: Video Conferencing and Webinars

Minimum

- ❑ Platform and materials are accessible to assistive tech
- ❑ Instructions for operation do not rely on senses
- ❑ Player controls can be used with the keyboard only
- ❑ NO KEYBOARD TRAPS!

Recommended

- ❑ Live captions are enabled
- ❑ Display orientation is not restricted
- ❑ Non-visual alternatives are available
- ❑ Non-audio alternatives are available
- ❑ Information is provided through multiple media
- ❑ Multiple and varied ways to participate
- ❑ Sensory stimulation and social demands are varied
- ❑ Mechanisms exist for cooperative learning

Advanced

- ❑ Provide prepared scripts for live audio content
- ❑ Provide alternatives for all media
- ❑ Provide sign language for audio content

Chapter 3:
Multimedia (Audio/Visual)

Podcasts and Audio Recordings
Recorded Webinars and Video Recordings
Images

Podcasts and Audio Recordings

What Do I Do?

Minimum

Ensure accessible materials and technologies to allow all learners to acquire the same information in an equally effective and usable way.

UDL Guideline 4.2: Optimize access to accessible materials and assistive and accessible technologies and tools

All audio content should have equivalent alternatives.

WCAG 3.0 – 2.1.2 Media Alternatives

Provide an alternative way for learners to access the information in prerecorded audio-only content. One way to do this is by providing a text transcript which contains the information learners need to understand the audio-only content.

WCAG 2.2 - 1.2.1 Audio-only and Video-only (Prerecorded)

Provide alternative text which allows screen readers to announce audio content before it begins playing.

WCAG 2.2 - 1.1.1 Non-text Content

For any audio content which starts automatically and lasts longer than three seconds, make sure that learners can pause or stop the audio and allow learners to adjust the volume.

WCAG 2.2 - 1.4.2 Audio Control

Make sure that audio player controls are usable with a keyboard or keyboard interface.

WCAG 2.2 - 2.1.1 Keyboard

Make sure that learners who navigate using a keyboard or keyboard interface can move focus away from all audio player controls. Also make sure this can be achieved using standard keyboard keys such as the 'Tab' or 'Arrow' keys, or that learners are made aware if they need to use non-standard keys.

WCAG 2.2 - 2.1.2 No Keyboard Trap

WCAG 3.0 – 2.4.1 Keyboard Interface Input

Recommended

Provide key information in a non-audio alternative, such as text transcripts, visual diagrams, or sign languages.

UDL Guideline 1.2: Support multiple ways to perceive information

Present key concepts in one medium with an alternative form available to aid comprehension.

UDL Guideline 2.5: Illustrate through multiple media

UDL Guideline 3.3: Cultivate multiple ways of knowing and making meaning

Advanced

For prerecorded audio-only content which has speech in the foreground and background audio, such as music, make sure the learner can switch off the background sounds. Another option is to make sure that background audio is approximately four times quieter than foreground audio.

WCAG. 1.4.7 Low or No Background Audio

Provide alternatives for all prerecorded media content.
WCAG 2.2 - 1.2.8 Media Alternative (Prerecorded)

Provide sign language interpretation for all prerecorded audio content.
WCAG 2.2 - 1.2.6 Sign Language (Prerecorded)

Who Benefits?

Learners with auditory disabilities (such as deafness, hard-of-hearing/ hearing loss, or auditory processing disorders) will face challenges with listening to audio content. Some learners may use assistive technology, such as hearing aids or personal listening devices, to access audio content.

Learners with cognitive impairments (learning and intellectual disabilities, for example) or neurodiversity (ADHD, autism spectrum, etc.) may also benefit from making audio content accessible. For example, those with sensory disabilities and learning disabilities may all require different ways of approaching content.

Some learners may grasp information quicker or more efficiently through visual or auditory means. Also, learning and transfer of learning occur when multiple representations are used, because these allow learners to make connections within, as well as between, concepts.

Checklist: Podcasts and Audio

Minimum

- ❑ Platform and materials are accessible to assistive tech
- ❑ Audio content has alternatives
- ❑ Audio content has a text transcript
- ❑ ALT text announces upcoming audio content
- ❑ Audio can be stopped and volume adjusted
- ❑ Audio control is available on keyboard
- ❑ Keyboard can change focus away from audio content

Recommended

- ❑ Non-audio alternatives are available
- ❑ Information is provided through multiple media

Advanced

- ❑ Background audio is removable or 4 times quieter
- ❑ Provide alternatives for all media
- ❑ Provide sign language for audio content

Recorded Webinars and Video Recordings

What Do I Do?

Minimum

Ensure accessible materials and technologies to allow all learners to acquire the same information in an equally effective and usable way.

UDL Guideline 4.2: Optimize access to accessible materials and assistive and accessible technologies and tools

All video content should have equivalent alternatives.

WCAG 3.0 – 2.1.2 Media Alternatives

Provide an alternative way for learners to access the information in prerecorded video content. Any video content with no audio track should also be described in text. One way to do this is by providing a text transcript which contains the information learners need to understand the audio or video content.

WCAG 2.2 - 1.2.1 Audio-only and Video-only (Prerecorded)

Provide descriptions (in either captions or a separate audio track) or text for important non-audio content in videos such as scene changes, actions, and expressions.

WCAG 2.2 - 1.2.3 Audio Description or Media Alternative (Prerecorded)

WCAG 3.0 – 2.1.5 Audio Descriptions

Provide alternative text which allows screen readers to announce video content before it begins playing.
WCAG 2.2 - 1.1.1 Non-text Content

For any video content which starts automatically and lasts longer than three seconds, make sure that learners can pause or stop the audio and allow learners to adjust the volume.
WCAG 2.2 - 1.4.2 Audio Control

Make sure that video player controls are usable with a keyboard or keyboard interface.
WCAG 2.2 - 2.1.1 Keyboard

Make sure that learners who navigate using a keyboard or keyboard interface can move focus away from all video player controls. Also make sure this can be achieved using standard keyboard keys such as the 'Tab' or 'Arrow' keys, or that learners are made aware if they need to use non-standard keys.
WCAG 2.2 - 2.1.2 No Keyboard Trap

Recommended

Provide audio descriptions which give all the information non-visual learners need to understand the video. This could include scene changes, actions, and expressions.
WCAG 2.2 – 1.2.5 Audio Description (Prerecorded)
WCAG 3.0 – 2.1.5 Audio Descriptions

Provide key information in a non-visual alternative, such as text, spoken descriptions, and other auditory cues.
UDL Guideline 1.3: Offer alternatives for visual information

Present key concepts in one medium with an alternative form available to aid comprehension.

UDL Guideline 2.5: Illustrate through multiple media

UDL Guideline 3.3: Cultivate multiple ways of knowing and making meaning

Advanced

Provide complete audio descriptions which give all the information non-visual learners need to understand the video, even if the video must pause to continue the audio description. This could include scene changes, actions, and expressions.

WCAG 2.2 - 1.2.7 Extended Audio Description (Prerecorded)

WCAG 3.0 - 2.1.5 Audio Descriptions

For prerecorded video content which has speech in the foreground and background audio, such as music, make sure the learner can switch off the background sounds. Another option is to make sure that background audio is approximately four times quieter than foreground audio.

WCAG 2.2 - 1.4.7 Low or No Background Audio

Provide alternatives for all prerecorded media content.

WCAG 2.2 - 1.2.8 Media Alternative (Prerecorded)

Provide sign language interpretation for all prerecorded audio content.

WCAG 2.2 - 1.2.6 Sign Language (Prerecorded)

Who Benefits?

Learners with auditory disabilities (such as deafness, hard-of-hearing/ hearing loss, or auditory processing disorders) will face challenges with video content that contains audio. Some learners may use assistive technology, such as hearing aids or personal listening devices, to access video content.

Learners with cognitive impairments (learning and intellectual disabilities, for example) or neurodiversity (ADHD, autism spectrum, etc.) may also benefit from making video content accessible. For example, those with sensory disabilities and learning disabilities may all require different ways of approaching content.

Some learners may grasp information quicker or more efficiently through visual or auditory means. Also, learning and transfer of learning occur when multiple representations are used, because these allow learners to make connections within, as well as between, concepts.

Checklist: Recorded Video

Minimum

- ❑ Platform and materials are accessible to assistive tech
- ❑ Video content has alternatives
- ❑ Video content has a text transcript
- ❑ Descriptions for important non-audio content
- ❑ ALT text announces upcoming video content
- ❑ Video can be stopped and volume adjusted
- ❑ Video control is available on keyboard
- ❑ Keyboard can change focus away from video content

Recommended

- ❑ Audio descriptions provide additional information
- ❑ Non-video alternatives are available
- ❑ Information is provided through multiple media

Advanced

- ❑ Video pauses to allow extended audio descriptions
- ❑ Background audio is removable or 4 times quieter
- ❑ Provide alternatives for all media
- ❑ Provide sign language for audio content

Images

What Do I Do?

Minimum

Ensure accessible materials and technologies to allow all learners to acquire the same information in an equally effective and usable way.

UDL Guideline 4.2: Optimize access to accessible materials and assistive and accessible technologies and tools

All images should have equivalent alternatives.

WCAG 3.0 – 2.1.1 Image Alternatives

Informative images should have descriptive alternative (ALT) text. Avoid using ALT text for purely decorative images. When writing alternative text, consider the following:

- When and where the photo was taken or created
- How many people are in the photo
- Basic description of actions and expressions
- Details like weather, signs, landmarks, etc.

WCAG 2.2 - 1.1.1 Non-text Content
EAPM Style & Accessibility Guide

Color should not be used as the only visual means of conveying information or distinguishing a visual element. Use icons, text, and other formatting to supplement color.

WCAG 2.2 - 1.4.1 Use of Color

Recommended

Avoid use of images of text, unless the image can be customized to the learner's needs or is essential to the meaning of the image, like text in a brand's logo.

WCAG 2.2 - 1.4.5 Images of Text

Make sure images and other important visuals have a contrast ratio of at least 3:1 against adjacent colors.

WCAG 2.2 - 1.4.11 Non-text Contrast

Do not restrict content views to a single display orientation, such as portrait or landscape, unless a specific display orientation is necessary to understand the meaning of the image, like sheet music or a personal check.

WCAG 2.2 - 1.3.4 Orientation

Provide key information in a non-visual alternative, such as text, spoken descriptions, and other auditory cues.

UDL Guideline 1.3: Offer alternatives for visual information

Present key concepts in one medium with an alternative form available to aid comprehension.

UDL Guideline 2.5: Illustrate through multiple media

UDL Guideline 3.3: Cultivate multiple ways of knowing and making meaning

Advanced

Use images of text only for decoration or when an image of text is essential, such as with a brand's logo.

WCAG 2.2 - 1.4.9 Images of Text (No Exception)

Who Benefits?

When images have ALT text, screen readers can produce a verbal description of the image, which allows learners with visual impairments to understand the image content.

Some learners with cognitive disabilities may have difficulty processing visual information. ALT text can provide a more concise and easier-to-understand description of an image, which can help learners understand the content of the image.

Some people with learning disabilities may have difficulty with reading comprehension. ALT text can provide a more concise and easier-to-understand description of an image, which can help learners understand the content of the image more efficiently.

Checklist: Images

Minimum

- ❑ Platform and materials are accessible to assistive tech
- ❑ Images have alternatives
- ❑ Informative images have useful ALT text
- ❑ Color is not the only way information is presented

Recommended

- ❑ Avoid images of text unless customizable or essential
- ❑ Display orientation is not restricted
- ❑ Non-visual alternatives are available
- ❑ Information is provided through multiple media

Advanced

- ❑ Use images of text only for decoration

Chapter 4: eLearning Modules

Navigation and Structure
Color and Font
Readability
Interactive Elements

Navigation and Structure

What Do I Do?

Minimum

Ensure accessible materials and technologies to allow all learners to acquire the same information in an equally effective and usable way.

UDL Guideline 4.2: Optimize access to accessible materials and assistive and accessible technologies and tools

Identify the language used in the eLearning resource so that assistive technology can read, display, and pronounce the language correctly.

WCAG 2.2 - 3.1.1 Language of Page

All pages or slides should have descriptive titles that make the topic or purpose of the page clear.

WCAG 2.2 - 2.4.2 Page Titled

Use headings and labels to provide clarity around how content is related. For example, an asterisk and red text indicate form fields that are required.

WCAG 2.2 - 1.3.1 Info and Relationships
WCAG 3.0 - 2.7.4 Structure

It should be clear where links will take the learner next, either from the link text itself or the context in the sentence leading up to the link.

WCAG 2.2 - 2.4.4 Link Purpose (In Context)

Make sure the visual presentation of the content matches what's read out by a screen reader by sequencing information correctly. If there are important alerts that appear elsewhere on the page (a cookie statement at the bottom of the page, for example, or anything else the learner must agree to before continuing), make sure they are sequenced to appear at the appropriate time to a screen reader.

WCAG 2.2 - 1.3.2 Meaningful Sequence

Make sure navigation sequences are presented in the correct order by applying a focus order that preserves both meaning and operability.

WCAG 2.2 - 2.4.3 Focus Order

Create a way to bypass blocks of content that are repeated across multiple pages or slides.

WCAG 2.2 - 2.4.1 Bypass Blocks

Make sure all content functionality is operable by the keyboard only. This does not forbid using the mouse or other input methods, but they should be in addition to keyboard functionality.

WCAG 2.2 - 2.1.1 Keyboard

WCAG 3.0 – 2.4.1 Keyboard Interface Input

If the keyboard focus can be moved to content on the slide using the keyboard interface, learners should also be able to move focus away from that content also using only the keyboard. If there is a non-standard exit method to remove focus from the content, the learner should be advised of this in advance. This is known commonly as a "keyboard trap," as it would "trap" a screen reader in a position it cannot get out of.

WCAG 2.2 - 2.1.2 No Keyboard Trap

WCAG 3.0 – 2.4.1 Keyboard Interface Input

Provide instructions for understanding and operating content that do not rely solely on sensory characteristics of components (such as shape, color, size, visual location, orientation, or sound).

WCAG 2.2 - 1.3.3 Sensory Characteristics

For any user interface components with labels that include text (such as text entry boxes), the name of the component should contain the same text that is represented visually.

WCAG 2.2 – 2.5.3 Label in Name

If your eLearning module has a help mechanism (including contact details or forms, FAQ pages, or automated systems), it should appear in the same place and in the same order on each page of content.

WCAG 2.2 – 3.2.6 Consistent Help

Recommended

Allow the learner to customize their visual layouts.

UDL Guideline 1.1: Support opportunities to customize the display of information

Provide multiple means of navigation and interaction with learning, including alternative input methods.

UDL Guideline 4.1: Vary and honor the methods for response, navigation, and movement

Give your learners multiple ways to navigate content or to locate a page, except for when content or pages must be followed in a locked sequence or are a step in a process.

WCAG 2.2 – 2.4.5 Multiple Ways

Navigation mechanisms (like a home or back button) that are repeated across multiple slides should appear in the same place and order each time.

WCAG 2.2 – 3.2.3 Consistent Navigation

Components that have the same functionality (like a submit button or search bar) are consistently identified.

WCAG 2.2 – 3.2.4 Consistent Identification

Use headings and labels that describe the topic or purpose of the section or page.

WCAG 2.2 - 2.4.6 Headings and Labels
WCAG 3.0 – 2.7.4 Structure

Identify the language used in each passage or phrase so that assistive technology can read, display, and pronounce the language correctly. Some exceptions include proper names and technical terms.

WCAG 2.2 – 3.1.2 Language of Parts

Do not restrict content views to a single display orientation, such as portrait or landscape, unless the orientation is essential to the meaning of the content.

WCAG 2.2 - 1.3.4 Orientation

Present content without loss of information or functionality by avoiding scrolling in two dimensions. The

best practice is to avoid scrolling within a width of 320 pixels and a height of 256 pixels.
WCAG 2.2 - 1.4.10 Reflow

Visible focus styling should indicate which element the learner is currently focused on.
WCAG 2.2 – 2.4.7 Focus Visible

If a mouse hover or keyboard focus reveals additional content, the content should be persistent until dismissed by the learner.
WCAG 2.2 - 1.4.13 Content on Hover or Focus
WCAG 3.0 – 2.3.1 Keyboard Focus Appearance
WCAG 3.0 – 2.4.2 Physical or Cognitive Effort When Using Keyboard

Status messages are programmed as such so that they may be presented to users of assistive technologies without receiving focus.
WCAG 2.2 – 4.1.3 Status Messages

Advanced

Use section headings to further organize content.
WCAG 2.2 – 2.4.10 Section Headings

Text-based instructions are provided so that intended actions are clear.
WCAG 2.2 – 3.3.5 Help

The purpose of links is clear from the link text alone. Avoid using phrases like “Read More” or “Click Here.”
WCAG 2.2 – 2.4.9 Link Purpose (Link Only)

EAPM Style & Accessibility Guide
Accessible Social

Information about the learner's location within the eLearning module is available and persistent.
WCAG 2.2 - 2.4.8 Location

A glossary or other mechanism exists to define unusual words, expand abbreviations, and assist with pronunciation if needed to understand context.
WCAG 2.2 - 3.1.3 Unusual Words
WCAG 2.2 - 3.1.4 Abbreviations
WCAG 2.2 - 3.1.6 Pronunciations
WCAG 3.0 - 2.2.3 Clear Language
UDL Guideline 2.1: Clarify vocabulary, symbols, and language structures
UDL Guideline 6.3: Organize information and resources

Who Benefits?

Learners with assistive technology benefit from a range of easy to implement design changes. Clear and consistent structure with logical headings, descriptive links, and keyboard navigation options enable learners to understand the content and move around the eLearning module efficiently.

Keyboard shortcuts, intuitive menu design, and other adjustments allow learners with limited dexterity to interact with the eLearning module without relying solely on a mouse.

Simple, organized layouts and predictable navigation patterns help learners with cognitive disabilities to process information and complete tasks.

Checklist: eLearning Navigation and Structure

Minimum

- ❑ Platform and materials are accessible to assistive tech
- ❑ Resource language is identified
- ❑ Slides have clear, descriptive titles
- ❑ Headings and labels indicate related content
- ❑ Links clearly indicate where they go
- ❑ Content is sequenced to show alerts in order
- ❑ Focus order reflects navigation order
- ❑ Repeated text can be bypassed
- ❑ All content can be used with keyboard only
- ❑ NO KEYBOARD TRAPS!
- ❑ Instructions for operation do not rely on senses
- ❑ UI components with text have matching labels
- ❑ FAQ and help pages appear in the same place

Recommended

- ❑ Layout is customizable by the learner
- ❑ Provide multiple ways to interact
- ❑ Allow multiple ways to navigate
- ❑ Navigation elements appear consistently
- ❑ Components with functionality are consistent
- ❑ Headings and labels describe topics and purpose
- ❑ Passage/phrase language(s) are identified
- ❑ Display orientation is not restricted
- ❑ Content display doesn't scroll
- ❑ Focus is visibly styled
- ❑ Additional content on hover is persistent
- ❑ Status messages are presented without focus

<u>Advanced</u>

- [ ] Content is further organized with section headings
- [ ] Instructions are provided as text only
- [ ] Link purpose is clear from link text alone
- [ ] Location information is persistent
- [ ] Glossary is available for definitions and pronunciation

Color and Font

What Do I Do?

Minimum

Provide instructions for understanding and operating content that do not rely solely on sensory characteristics of components (such as shape, color, size, visual location, orientation, or sound).

WCAG 2.2 - 1.3.3 Sensory Characteristics

Do not use color as the only visual means of conveying information, indicating an action, prompting a response, or distinguishing a visual element. Use icons, text, and other formatting to supplement color.

WCAG 2.2 - 1.4.1 Use of Color

Recommended

Allow the learner to customize their text size, contrast, colors, and fonts.

UDL Guideline 1.1: Support opportunities to customize the display of information

Choose dark colored text on a light colored (not white) background, when possible, for improved readability.

The Dyslexia-Friendly Style Guide

Use single color backgrounds, avoiding patterns or pictures which can distract from important context.

The Dyslexia-Friendly Style Guide

Use a contrast ratio of at least 4.5:1 for visual presentation of text and images of text. When the text is large-scale, use a contrast ratio of at least 3:1.
WCAG 2.2 - 1.4.3 Contrast (Minimum)

For graphical objects and interface components, use a contrast ratio of at least 3:1 against adjacent colors.
WCAG 2.2 - 1.4.11 Non-text Contrast

When setting your font styles, do the following:

- Use sans-serif fonts such as Arial, Verdana, and Open Sans so that text appears less crowded.
- Font size should be no smaller than 12pt.
- Headings should be at least 20% larger than surrounding text and are often presented **bold**.

The Dyslexia-Friendly Style Guide
WCAG 3.0 - 2.2.1 Text Appearance

Use **bold** text for emphasis instead of *italics* or underlining, which can make text appear crowded.
The Dyslexia-Friendly Style Guide

Avoid using ALL CAPITAL LETTERS, especially in titles, as this can be more difficult for learners to read than Sentence Case.
The Dyslexia-Friendly Style Guide
Accessible Social
WCAG 3.0 - 2.2.1 Text Appearance

When setting your text styles, do the following:

- Line height is at least 1.5 times the font size.
- Paragraph spacing is at least 2 times the font size.

- Letter spacing is at least 0.12 times the font size.
- Word spacing is at least 0.16 times the font size.
- Word spacing is at least 3.5 times letter spacing.

WCAG 2.2 - 1.4.12 Text Spacing
WCAG 3.0 – 2.2.1 Text Appearance
The Dyslexia-Friendly Style Guide

Ensure that text can be resized without assistive technology - up to 200% without loss of content or functionality. Captions and images of text are exceptions.
WCAG 2.2 - 1.4.4 Resize Text

Avoid use of images of text, unless the image can be customized to the learner's needs or is essential to the meaning of the image, like text in a brand's logo.
WCAG 2.2 - 1.4.5 Images of Text

Avoid "fancy font" generators and other tools that replace text with Unicode symbols. These are either translated into different languages, read unintelligibly, or skipped entirely by screen readers.
Accessible Social

Advanced

Use images of text only for decoration or when an image of text is essential, such as with a brand's logo.
WCAG 2.2 - 1.4.9 Images of Text (No Exception)

Use a contrast ratio of at least 7:1 for visual presentation of text and images of text. When the text is large-scale, use a contrast ratio of at least 4.5:1.
WCAG 2.2 - 1.4.6 Contrast (Enhanced)

When a focus indicator is visible, it has a contrast ratio of at least 3:1 between focused and unfocused states, and is outlined at least 2px thick.
WCAG 2.2 - 2.4.13 Focus Appearance

When presenting blocks of text visually, ensure the following:

- The width of the block is no more than 80 characters (or 40 if logographic characters, such as Japanese or Hieroglyphics).
- Avoid multiple columns of text.
- Text is aligned to the left, right, or center - not justified (aligned to both the left and right, creating uneven spaces between words). Left alignment is preferred, unless the reading direction of the language differs.
- Line spacing is at least 1.5 within paragraphs, and paragraph spacing is 1.5 times larger than line spacing.
- Text can be resized without assistive technology - up to 200% without loss of content or functionality - and without requiring the learner to scroll horizontally on a full-screen window.
- Foreground and background colors can be selected by the learner.

WCAG 2.2 - 1.4.8 Visual Presentation
WCAG 3.0 – 2.2.1 Text Appearance
The Dyslexia-Friendly Style Guide

Avoid using *italic*, underlined, or **bold** text to convey emphasis, as these are not able to be read by screen readers. Instead, convey the emphasis through text. (She emphasized the document was available to anyone.)

EAPM Style & Accessibility Guide

WCAG 3.0 – 2.2.1 Text Appearance

Who Benefits?

Adjustments to colors and fonts primarily benefit learners with vision impairments, however there is also a great benefit to learners with other cognitive limitations. High contrast between text and background is crucial for learners with low vision or color blindness. Simple color palettes and consistent font styles throughout the eLearning module reduce cognitive overload for people with learning disabilities or attention difficulties. Adequate space between lines and paragraphs improves readability, especially for learners with dyslexia or visual processing difficulties.

Checklist: eLearning Color and Font

Minimum

- ❑ Instructions for operation do not rely on senses
- ❑ Color is not the only way information is presented

Recommended

- ❑ Learner can customize color and font settings
- ❑ Use light backgrounds with dark text
- ❑ Use single color background (not patterns)
- ❑ Text contrast is 4.5:1 for standard, 3:1 for large text
- ❑ UI components have 3:1 contrast to nearby objects
- ❑ Use a sans-serif font of at least 12pt
- ❑ Headings are at least 20% larger than nearby text
- ❑ **Bold** is used for emphasis instead of underline or *italic*
- ❑ Use Sentence Case NOT ALL CAPS
- ❑ Text line height is at 1.5
- ❑ Spacing after paragraphs is at 2.0
- ❑ Letter spacing is at least 0.12 times the font size
- ❑ Word spacing is at least 0.16 times the font size and 3.5 times the letter spacing
- ❑ Text can be resized without assistive technology
- ❑ Avoid images of text unless customizable or essential
- ❑ Avoid "fancy fonts"

Advanced

- ❑ Use images of text only for decoration
- ❑ Text contrast is 7:1 for standard, 4.5:1 for large text
- ❑ Focus indicator is 2px outline and 3:1 contrast
- ❑ Text blocks are no more than 80 characters wide
- ❑ Text does not appear in columns

- ❑ Text is primarily left aligned
- ❑ Paragraph spacing is at least 1.5 times line spacing
- ❑ Text can be resized without requiring scrolling
- ❑ Learner can select foreground and background colors
- ❑ Avoid using formatting to emphasize text

Readability

What Do I Do?

Minimum

Identify the language used in the eLearning resource so that assistive technology can read, display, and pronounce the language correctly.

WCAG 2.2 - 3.1.1 Language of Page

All pages or slides should have descriptive titles that make the topic or purpose of the page clear.

WCAG 2.2 - 2.4.2 Page Titled

Use headings and labels to provide clarity around how content is related.

WCAG 2.2 - 1.3.1 Info and Relationships
WCAG 3.0 – 2.7.4 Structure

It should be clear where links will take the learner next, either from the link text itself or the context in the sentence leading up to the link.

WCAG 2.2 – 2.4.4 Link Purpose (In Context)

Make sure the visual presentation of the content matches what's read out by a screen reader by sequencing information correctly.

WCAG 2.2 - 1.3.2 Meaningful Sequence

Recommended

Use headings and labels that describe the topic or purpose of the section or page.

WCAG 2.2 - 2.4.6 Headings and Labels
WCAG 3.0 – 2.7.4 Structure

Identify the language used in each passage or phrase so that assistive technology can read, display, and pronounce the language correctly. Some exceptions include proper names and technical terms.
WCAG 2.2 – 3.1.2 Language of Parts

Consider your word usage:

- Write in the active voice instead of passive voice.
- Choose short, simple words that are common and easy to understand.
- Use contractions as appropriate.
- Omit unnecessary words.

Federal Plain Language Guidelines
ISO 24495-1:2023 Plain Language

Consider your sentence structure:

- Avoid run-on sentences. Use clear, short sentences and paragraphs.
- Avoid double negatives.
- Place main ideas before exceptions and conditions.
- Use transition words between paragraphs.
- Write short paragraphs with one main idea each.

Federal Plain Language Guidelines
ISO 24495-1:2023 Plain Language

Use aids to clarify meaning, such as diagrams, tables, and illustrations.
Federal Plain Language Guidelines
ISO 24495-1:2023 Plain Language

Use parentheses sparingly and try to reword your sentences to avoid using them. These are generally not read by screen readers and may create unintended sentence structures when omitted.

EAPM Style & Accessibility Guide

Advanced

Use section headings to further organize content.

WCAG 2.2 – 2.4.10 Section Headings
WCAG 3.0 – 2.7.4 Structure

Text-based instructions are provided so that intended actions are clear.

WCAG 2.2 – 3.3.5 Help

The purpose of links is clear from the link text alone. Avoid using phrases like “Read More” or “Click Here.”

WCAG 2.2 – 2.4.9 Link Purpose (Link Only)
EAPM Style & Accessibility Guide

Text should be readable at the 9th grade level after removing proper names and titles, or an alternate version of the text should be available that meets this recommendation. Consider Plain English and Easy English formats.

WCAG 2.2 – 3.1.5 Reading Level
Centre for Inclusive Design
Easy Read Australia
ISO 24495-1:2023 Plain Language
Accessible Social

A glossary or other mechanism exists to define unusual words, expand abbreviations, and assist with pronunciation if needed to understand context.

WCAG 2.2 - 3.1.3 Unusual Words

WCAG 2.2 - 3.1.4 Abbreviations

WCAG 2.2 - 3.1.6 Pronunciations

WCAG 3.0 - 2.2.3 Clear Language

UDL Guideline 2.1: Clarify vocabulary, symbols, and language structures

UDL Guideline 6.3: Organize information and resources

Who Benefits?

Readability makes information easier to process and understand. Simple sentence structures and familiar terms reduce cognitive load, improving comprehension and retention. This is particularly helpful for learners with cognitive impairments or learning disabilities like dyslexia.

For learners with low vision or blindness, plain language can make text easier to interpret and navigate.

Learners with hearing impairments often rely on written communication. Plain language ensures they can access information effectively, especially when instructions, procedures, or important details are involved.

Checklist: eLearning Readability

Minimum

- ❑ Page language is identified
- ❑ Pages have clear, descriptive titles
- ❑ Headings and labels indicate related content
- ❑ Links clearly indicate where they go
- ❑ Content is sequenced in order for screen readers

Recommended

- ❑ Headings and labels describe topics and purpose
- ❑ Passage/phrase language(s) are identified
- ❑ Write in active voice
- ❑ Choose short, simple words
- ❑ Use contractions
- ❑ Omit unnecessary words
- ❑ Use clear, short sentences
- ❑ Avoid double negatives
- ❑ Place main ideas first, then exceptions
- ❑ Use transition words
- ❑ Have one main idea per paragraph
- ❑ Use diagrams and tables to clarify meaning
- ❑ Avoid using parentheses if possible

Advanced

- ❑ Content is further organized with section headings
- ❑ Instructions are provided as text only
- ❑ Link purpose is clear from link text alone
- ❑ Text is readable at 9th grade level (or alternate format)
- ❑ Glossary is available for definitions and pronunciation

Interactive Elements

What Do I Do?

Minimum

Ensure accessible materials and technologies to allow all learners to acquire the same information in an equally effective and usable way.

UDL Guideline 4.2: Optimize access to accessible materials and assistive and accessible technologies and tools

Provide instructions for understanding and operating content that do not rely solely on sensory characteristics of components (such as shape, color, size, visual location, orientation, or sound).

WCAG 2.2 - 1.3.3 Sensory Characteristics

Do not use color as the only visual means of conveying information, indicating an action, prompting a response, or distinguishing a visual element. Use icons, text, and other formatting to supplement color.

WCAG 2.2 - 1.4.1 Use of Color

Interactive elements (such as buttons) should have descriptive alternative (ALT) text. Avoid using ALT text for purely decorative content.

WCAG 2.2 - 1.1.1 Non-text Content

Interactive elements should have accessible and meaningful names, states, and roles.

WCAG 2.2 – 4.1.2 Name, Role, Value

The learner can always access help during the interaction, such as an instruction slide or an email address to contact for help.

WCAG 2.2 – 3.2.6 Consistent Help

Labels, instructions, or other help text are provided to prevent triggering an error on required learner input.

WCAG 2.2 – 3.3.2 Labels or Instructions
WCAG 3.0 – 2.5.1 Correct Errors
WCAG 3.0 – 2.5.2 Prevent Errors

Any error messages are communicated in text and provide instructions on how to proceed.

WCAG 2.2 – 3.3.1 Error Identification
WCAG 3.0 – 2.5.1 Correct Errors
WCAG 3.0 – 2.5.2 Prevent Errors

No unexpected changes happen to content when it receives focus.

WCAG 2.2 – 3.2.1 On Focus

No unexpected changes happen to content when it receives learner input.

WCAG 2.2 – 3.2.2 On Input

Make sure navigation sequences are presented in the correct order by applying a focus order that preserves both meaning and operability.

WCAG 2.2 - 2.4.3 Focus Order

Previously entered information can be auto-populated or available to select, unless re-entering the information is part

of the interaction or the information is no longer valid.
WCAG 2.2 – 3.3.7 Redundant Entry

Make sure all content functionality is operable by the keyboard only. This does not forbid using the mouse or other input methods, but they should be in addition to keyboard functionality.
WCAG 2.2 - 2.1.1 Keyboard
WCAG 3.0 – 2.4.1 Keyboard Interface Input

If the keyboard focus can be moved using the keyboard interface, learners should also be able to move focus away also using only the keyboard. If there is a non-standard exit method to remove focus from the content, the learner should be advised of this in advance. This is known commonly as a “keyboard trap,” as it would “trap” a screen reader in a position it cannot get out of.
WCAG 2.2 - 2.1.2 No Keyboard Trap
WCAG 3.0 – 2.4.1 Keyboard Interface Input
WCAG 3.0 – 2.4.2 Physical or Cognitive Effort When Using Keyboard

If keyboard shortcuts (any combination of letters, numbers, and symbols) are implemented as part of your interaction, these shortcuts can either be turned off, remapped, or activated only when content is focused. Custom keyboard shortcuts can interfere with functions of assistive technology.
WCAG 2.2 - 2.1.4 Character Key Shortcuts

All actions that are carried out using a gesture (such as swiping, pinching, or drawing) can also be done with a button or buttons.

WCAG 2.2 - 2.5.1 Pointer Gestures
WCAG 3.0 - 2.4.3 Pointer Input

Actions are triggered on mouse-up instead of on mouse-down, or a mechanism exists to undo the learner's choice.

WCAG 2.2 - 2.5.2 Pointer Cancellation
WCAG 3.0 - 2.4.3 Pointer Input

For any media content which starts automatically and lasts longer than three seconds, make sure that learners can pause or stop the audio and allow learners to adjust the volume.

WCAG 2.2 - 1.4.2 Audio Control

When time limits are set on content or interactions, the learner should be able to extend, adjust, or turn off the time limit. The only exception is when a timed activity is a critical part of the learning exercise.

WCAG 2.2 - 2.2.1 Timing Adjustable

For any content that moves, blinks, scrolls, or auto-updates and starts automatically, allow the learner to pause, stop, or hide this content unless it is essential to the activity.

WCAG 2.2 - 2.2.2 Pause, Stop, Hide

Device motion (such as shaking or tilting) is not required to complete the interaction.

WCAG 2.2 - 2.5.4 Motion Actuation
WCAG 3.0 - 2.6.1 Avoid Physical Harm

Interactions do not contain elements that flash more than 3 times per second, or the flash occupies a fraction of the slide (25% of any 10° visual field).

WCAG 2.2 – 2.3.1 Three Flashes or Below Threshold

WCAG 3.0 – 2.6.1 Avoid Physical Harm

Recommended

Visible focus styling should indicate which element the learner is currently focused on.

WCAG 2.2 – 2.4.7 Focus Visible

When an element receives focus, it is not completely hidden by other content.

WCAG 2.2 – 2.4.11 Focus Not Obscured (Minimum)

WCAG 3.0 – 2.7.5 No Obstruction

If a mouse hover or keyboard focus reveals additional content, the content should be hoverable without disappearing, dismissible if it obscures other content, and persistent until dismissed by the learner.

WCAG 2.2 – 1.4.13 Content on Hover or Focus

WCAG 3.0 – 2.3.1 Keyboard Focus Appearance

WCAG 3.0 – 2.4.2 Physical or Cognitive Effort When Using Keyboard

WCAG 3.0 – 2.7.5 No Obstruction

Dragging movements are avoided or an alternative method is provided (such as button or mouse input) to complete the interaction.

WCAG 2.2 – 2.5.7 Dragging Movements

WCAG 3.0 – 2.6.1 Avoid Physical Harm

Any element that can be selected as a target should be at least 24 by 24 pixels.

WCAG 2.2 - 2.5.8 Target Size (Minimum)

Provide key information in a non-visual alternative, such as spoken descriptions or other auditory cues.

UDL Guideline 1.2: Support multiple ways to perceive information

Provide key information in a non-audio alternative, such as text transcripts or sign languages.

UDL Guideline 1.2: Support multiple ways to perceive information

Present key concepts in one medium with an alternative form available to aid comprehension.

UDL Guideline 2.5: Illustrate through multiple media

UDL Guideline 3.3: Cultivate multiple ways of knowing and making meaning

Provide multiple means of navigation and interaction with learning, including alternative input methods.

UDL Guideline 4.1: Vary and honor the methods for response, navigation, and movement

Provide multiple forms of expression of communication, such as offering the choice between text or speech responses, or incorporating interactivity such as social media and annotation tools.

UDL Guideline 5.1: Use multiple media for communication

Allow for multiple and varied ways of participating and demonstrating understanding.

UDL Guideline 5.4: Address biases related to modes of expression and communication

Advanced

All interactivity can be operated using the keyboard only, without requiring timed keystrokes as part of the interaction

WCAG 2.2 - 2.1.3 Keyboard (No Exception)

When an element receives focus, no part of it is hidden by other content.

WCAG 2.2 - 2.4.11 Focus Not Obscured (Enhanced)
WCAG 3.0 - 2.7.5 No Obstruction

When a focus indicator is visible, it has a contrast ratio of at least 3:1 between focused and unfocused states, and is outlined at least 2px thick.

WCAG 2.2 - 2.4.13 Focus Appearance

Any element that can be selected as a target should be at least 44 by 44 pixels.

WCAG 2.2 - 2.5.5 Target Size (Enhanced)

The learner should be able to check their responses before submitting, and be able to reverse the submission and make edits after submitting, unless it would otherwise invalidate the interaction.

WCAG 2.2 - 3.3.6 Error Prevention
WCAG 3.0 - 2.5.1 Correct Errors
WCAG 3.0 - 2.5.2 Prevent Errors

Learners are warned if their inactivity could cause loss of information or progress.
WCAG 2.2 - 2.2.6 Timeouts

Timing is not an essential part of the interaction.
WCAG 2.2 - 2.2.3 No Timing

For prerecorded media content which has speech in the foreground and background audio, such as music, make sure the learner can switch off the background sounds. Another option is to make sure that background audio is approximately four times quieter than foreground audio.
WCAG 2.2 - 1.4.7 Low or No Background Audio

Provide alternatives for all prerecorded media content.
WCAG 2.2 - 1.2.8 Media Alternative (Prerecorded)

Interactions do not contain elements that flash more than 3 times per second.
WCAG 2.2 - 2.3.1 Three Flashes
WCAG 3.0 - 2.6.1 Avoid Physical Harm

Interactions with triggered motion animations can be disabled, unless the animation is essential to the activity.
WCAG 2.2 - 2.3.3 Animation from Interactions
WCAG 3.0 - 2.6.1 Avoid Physical Harm

Who Benefits?

Learners with vision impairments may use screen readers, which require compatible interfaces and interactions with clear navigation elements and keyboard controls.

Learners with motor disabilities may use features like keyboard navigation, voice control, and alternative input methods like joysticks or eye tracking to interact with the eLearning module without a mouse.

For learners with cognitive or learning disabilities, timed activities with adjustable intervals and frequent progress checks can support focus and motivation.

Features like adjustable flashing animations and alternative content formats are important to avoid potential triggers for epilepsy and photosensitivity.

Checklist: eLearning Interactions

Minimum

- ❑ Platform and materials are accessible to assistive tech
- ❑ Instructions for operation do not rely on senses
- ❑ Color is not the only way information is presented
- ❑ Interactive elements have descriptive ALT text
- ❑ Interactive elements have meaningful names
- ❑ Help slides or references appear in the same place
- ❑ Instructions to prevent errors are provided as text
- ❑ Error messages are informative and provided as text
- ❑ Nothing unexpected happens on focus change
- ❑ Nothing unexpected happens on input
- ❑ Focus order reflects navigation order
- ❑ Previously entered information is available
- ❑ All content can be used with the keyboard only
- ❑ NO KEYBOARD TRAPS!
- ❑ Avoid custom keyboard shortcuts
- ❑ Gesture actions can also be done with a button
- ❑ Actions trigger on mouse-up, not mouse-down
- ❑ Media can be stopped and volume adjusted
- ❑ Time limits can be extended, adjusted, or turned off
- ❑ Content that moves can be stopped or hidden
- ❑ Device motion is not required
- ❑ No more than 3 flashes per second, unless on a small part of the slide

Recommended

- ❑ Focus is visibly styled
- ❑ Focused elements are not completely hidden
- ❑ Additional content on hover is persistent

- ❑ Dragging movements are avoided
- ❑ Anything targetable is at least 24x24 px
- ❑ Non-visual alternatives are available
- ❑ Non-audio alternatives are available
- ❑ Information is provided through multiple media
- ❑ Provide multiple ways to interact
- ❑ Multiple media are used for interaction
- ❑ Multiple and varied ways to participate

Advanced

- ❑ Resource operates with keyboard only, without timed keystrokes as part of the interaction
- ❑ No parts of focused elements are hidden
- ❑ Focus indicator is 2px outline and 3:1 contrast
- ❑ Anything targetable is at least 44x44 px
- ❑ Learner can check responses before submitting, and reverse the submission if possible
- ❑ Provide warnings of information loss due to inactivity
- ❑ Timing is not part of the activity
- ❑ Background audio is removable or 4 times quieter
- ❑ Provide alternatives for all media
- ❑ Nothing flashes more than 3 times per second
- ❑ Animations can be disabled unless essential

Chapter 5: Digital Reference Material

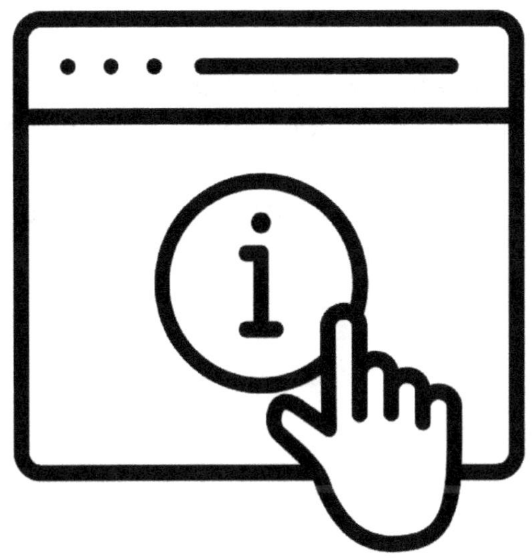

Adobe PDFs
Microsoft Word/PowerPoint
Navigation and Structure
Color and Font
Readability

Digital Reference

This chapter contains everything else you might be creating for online learning. There are accessibility recommendations for specific types of documents, but also overall principles that apply to any type of digital reference material.

If your digital reference is part of an intranet or website, you will find the Asynchronous Learning Platforms chapter valuable for setting up the platform which contains these documents. This chapter focuses on the accessibility of digital documents themselves.

Adobe PDF (Portable Document Format)

What Do I Do?

Minimum

Adobe products have a built-in accessibility checker to help you identify potential accessibility issues and suggest improvements. In the current versions of these products, this tool is located under the Tools menu.

Ensure accessible materials and technologies to allow all learners to acquire the same information in an equally effective and usable way.

UDL Guideline 4.2: Optimize access to accessible materials and assistive and accessible technologies and tools

Ensure your document can be navigated using only the keyboard.

WCAG 2.2 - 2.1.1 Keyboard

Recommended

As files can be rather large depending on their content, it is helpful to learners to include information pre-download about the document contents and file size.

Federal Plain Language Guidelines

ISO 24495-1:2023 Plain Language

Apply or create built-in styles instead of manually formatting text to ensure better document structure.

The Dyslexia-Friendly Style Guide

Create and use accessible templates with appropriate colors, contrast, fonts, and text spacing.

Use bullet points, large fonts, and "white space" to keep your document organized and readable.
The Dyslexia-Friendly Style Guide
Federal Plain Language Guidelines
ISO 24495-1:2023 Plain Language

Advanced

Add document metadata (author, title, keywords, etc.) to improve access and storage of documents.

Microsoft Word / PowerPoint

What Do I Do?

Minimum

Microsoft products have a built-in accessibility checker to help you identify potential accessibility issues and suggest improvements. In the current versions of these products, this tool is located under the Review menu.

Ensure accessible materials and technologies to allow all learners to acquire the same information in an equally effective and usable way.

UDL Guideline 4.2: Optimize access to accessible materials and assistive and accessible technologies and tools

Ensure your document can be navigated using only the keyboard.

WCAG 2.2 - 2.1.1 Keyboard

Recommended

Apply or create built-in styles instead of manually formatting text to ensure better document structure.

The Dyslexia-Friendly Style Guide

Create and use accessible templates with appropriate colors, contrast, fonts, and text spacing.

Use bullet points, large fonts, and “white space” to keep your document organized and readable.

The Dyslexia-Friendly Style Guide

Federal Plain Language Guidelines
ISO 24495-1:2023 Plain Language

Advanced

Add document metadata (author, title, keywords, etc.) to improve access and storage of documents.

Who Benefits?

Learners with assistive technology benefit from a range of easy to implement document changes. Accessible documents allow for compatibility with screen readers and other assistive technology. Features like enhanced color contrast, adjustable font size, and alternative text descriptions for images improve readability.

For those with cognitive and learning disabilities, structured documents with clear formatting, logical hierarchy, and consistent layout aid in information processing. Concise and well-organized content minimizes distractions and supports focus.

Checklist: Specific Document Types

Minimum

- [ ] Run the built-in accessibility tool
- [ ] Materials are accessible to assistive tech
- [ ] Test navigation with keyboard only

Recommended

- [ ] Provide document information before download
- [ ] Use styles for formatting
- [ ] Use accessible templates
- [ ] Organize with white space and bullets

Advanced

- [ ] Add document metadata

Navigation and Structure

What Do I Do?

Minimum

Ensure accessible materials and technologies to allow all learners to acquire the same information in an equally effective and usable way.

UDL Guideline 4.2: Optimize access to accessible materials and assistive and accessible technologies and tools

Identify the language used in the document so that assistive technology can read, display, and pronounce the language correctly.

WCAG 2.2 – 3.1.1 Language of Page

All documents should have descriptive titles that make the topic or purpose of the file clear.

WCAG 2.2 - 2.4.2 Page Titled

Use headings and labels to provide clarity around how content is related. For example, an asterisk and red text indicates form fields that are required.

WCAG 2.2 - 1.3.1 Info and Relationships
WCAG 3.0 – 2.7.4 Structure

It should be clear where links will take the learner next, either from the link text itself or the context in the sentence leading up to the link.

WCAG 2.2 – 2.4.4 Link Purpose (In Context)

Make sure the visual presentation of the content matches what's read out by a screen reader by sequencing information correctly.

WCAG 2.2 - 1.3.2 Meaningful Sequence

Provide instructions for understanding and operating content that do not rely solely on sensory characteristics of components (such as shape, color, size, visual location, orientation, or sound).

WCAG 2.2 - 1.3.3 Sensory Characteristics

Recommended

Use headings and labels that describe the topic or purpose of the section or page.

WCAG 2.2 - 2.4.6 Headings and Labels
WCAG 3.0 – 2.7.4 Structure

Identify the language used in each passage or phrase so that assistive technology can read, display, and pronounce the language correctly. Some exceptions include proper names and technical terms.

WCAG 2.2 – 3.1.2 Language of Parts

Do not restrict content views to a single display orientation, such as portrait or landscape, unless the orientation is essential to the meaning of the content.

WCAG 2.2 - 1.3.4 Orientation

Advanced

Use section headings to further organize content.
WCAG 2.2 - 2.4.10 Section Headings
WCAG 3.0 - 2.7.4 Structure

Text-based instructions are provided so that intended actions are clear.
WCAG 2.2 - 3.3.5 Help

The purpose of links is clear from the link text alone. Avoid using phrases like "Read More" or "Click Here."
WCAG 2.2 - 2.4.9 Link Purpose (Link Only)
EAPM Style & Accessibility Guide
Accessible Social

A glossary or other mechanism exists to define unusual words, expand abbreviations, and assist with pronunciation if needed to understand context.
WCAG 2.2 - 3.1.3 Unusual Words
WCAG 2.2 - 3.1.4 Abbreviations
WCAG 2.2 - 3.1.6 Pronunciations
WCAG 3.0 - 2.2.3 Clear Language
UDL Guideline 2.1: Clarify vocabulary, symbols, and language structures
UDL Guideline 6.3: Organize information and resources

Who Benefits?

Learners with assistive technology benefit from a range of easy to implement document changes. Clear and consistent page structure with logical headings, descriptive links, and keyboard navigation options enable learners to understand the content and move around the document efficiently.

Simple, organized layouts and predictable navigation patterns help learners with cognitive disabilities to process information and complete tasks.

Checklist: Document Navigation and Structure

Minimum

- ❑ Materials are accessible to assistive tech
- ❑ Document language is identified
- ❑ Documents have clear, descriptive titles
- ❑ Headings and labels indicate related content
- ❑ Links clearly indicate where they go
- ❑ Instructions for operation do not rely on senses

Recommended

- ❑ Headings and labels describe topics and purpose
- ❑ Passage/phrase language(s) are identified
- ❑ Display orientation is not restricted

Advanced

- ❑ Content is further organized with section headings
- ❑ Instructions are provided as text only
- ❑ Link purpose is clear from link text alone
- ❑ Glossary is available for definitions and pronunciation

Color and Font

What Do I Do?

Minimum

Provide instructions for understanding and operating content that do not rely solely on sensory characteristics of components (such as shape, color, size, visual location, orientation, or sound).

WCAG 2.2 - 1.3.3 Sensory Characteristics

Do not use color as the only visual means of conveying information, indicating an action, prompting a response, or distinguishing a visual element. Use icons, text, and other formatting to supplement color.

WCAG 2.2 - 1.4.1 Use of Color

Recommended

Allow the learner to customize their text size, contrast, colors, and fonts.

UDL Guideline 1.1: Support opportunities to customize the display of information

Choose dark colored text on a light colored (not white) background, when possible, for improved readability.

The Dyslexia-Friendly Style Guide

Use single color backgrounds, avoiding patterns or pictures which can distract from important context.

The Dyslexia-Friendly Style Guide

Use a contrast ratio of at least 4.5:1 for visual presentation of text and images of text. When the text is large-scale, use a contrast ratio of at least 3:1.

WCAG 2.2 - 1.4.3 Contrast (Minimum)

For graphical objects and interface components, use a contrast ratio of at least 3:1 against adjacent colors.

WCAG 2.2 - 1.4.11 Non-text Contrast

When setting your font styles, do the following:

- Use sans-serif fonts such as Arial, Verdana, and Open Sans so that text appears less crowded.
- Font size should be no smaller than 12pt.
- Headings should be at least 20% larger than surrounding text and are often presented **bold**.

The Dyslexia-Friendly Style Guide

WCAG 3.0 - 2.2.1 Text Appearance

Use **bold** text for emphasis instead of *italics* or underlining, which can make text appear crowded.

The Dyslexia-Friendly Style Guide

Avoid using ALL CAPITAL LETTERS, especially in titles, as this can be more difficult for learners to read than Sentence Case.

The Dyslexia-Friendly Style Guide

WCAG 3.0 - 2.2.1 Text Appearance

When setting your text styles, do the following:

- Line height is at least 1.5 times the font size.
- Spacing after paragraphs is at least 2 times the font size.

- Letter spacing is at least 0.12 times the font size.
- Word spacing is at least 0.16 times the font size.
- Word spacing is at least 3.5 times letter spacing.

WCAG 2.2 - 1.4.12 Text Spacing
WCAG 3.0 – 2.2.1 Text Appearance
The Dyslexia-Friendly Style Guide

Ensure that text can be resized without assistive technology - up to 200% without loss of content or functionality. Captions and images of text are exceptions.
WCAG 2.2 - 1.4.4 Resize Text

Avoid use of images of text, unless the image can be customized to the learner's needs or is essential to the meaning of the image, like text in a brand's logo.
WCAG 2.2 - 1.4.5 Images of Text

<u>Advanced</u>

Use images of text only for decoration or when an image of text is essential, such as with a brand's logo.
WCAG 2.2 - 1.4.9 Images of Text (No Exception)

Use a contrast ratio of at least 7:1 for visual presentation of text and images of text. When the text is large-scale, use a contrast ratio of at least 4.5:1.
WCAG 2.2 - 1.4.6 Contrast (Enhanced)

When presenting blocks of text visually, do the following:

- The width of the block is no more than 80 characters (or 40 if logographic characters, such as Japanese or Hieroglyphics).
- Avoid multiple columns of text.

- Text is aligned to the left, right, or center - not justified (aligned to both the left and right, creating uneven spaces between words). Left alignment is preferred, unless the reading direction of the language differs.
- Line spacing is at least 1.5 within paragraphs, and paragraph spacing is 1.5 times larger than line spacing.
- Text can be resized without assistive technology - up to 200% without loss of content or functionality - and without requiring the learner to scroll horizontally on a full-screen window.
- Foreground and background colors can be selected by the learner.

WCAG 2.2 - 1.4.8 Visual Presentation
WCAG 3.0 – 2.2.1 Text Appearance
The Dyslexia-Friendly Style Guide

Avoid using *italic*, underlined, or **bold** text to convey emphasis, as these are not able to be read by screen readers. Instead, convey the emphasis through text. (She emphasized the document was available to anyone.)
EAPM Style & Accessibility Guide
WCAG 3.0 – 2.2.1 Text Appearance

Who Benefits?

Adjustments to colors and fonts primarily benefit learners with vision impairments, however there is also a great benefit to learners with other cognitive limitations. High contrast between text and background is crucial for learners with low vision or color blindness. Simple color palettes and consistent font styles throughout the platform reduce cognitive overload for people with learning disabilities or attention difficulties. Adequate space between lines and paragraphs improves readability, especially for learners with dyslexia or visual processing difficulties.

Checklist: Document Color and Font

Minimum

- ❑ Instructions for operation do not rely on senses
- ❑ Color is not the only way information is presented

Recommended

- ❑ Learner can customize color and font settings
- ❑ Use light backgrounds with dark text
- ❑ Use single color background (not patterns)
- ❑ Text contrast is 4.5:1 for standard, 3:1 for large text
- ❑ UI components have 3:1 contrast to nearby objects
- ❑ Use a sans-serif font of at least 12pt
- ❑ Headings are at least 20% larger than nearby text
- ❑ **Bold** is used for emphasis instead of underline or *italic*
- ❑ Use Sentence Case NOT ALL CAPS
- ❑ Text line height is at 1.5
- ❑ Spacing after paragraphs is at 2.0
- ❑ Letter spacing is at least 0.12 times the font size
- ❑ Word spacing is at least 0.16 times the font size and 3.5 times the letter spacing
- ❑ Text can be resized without assistive technology
- ❑ Avoid images of text unless customizable or essential

Advanced

- ❑ Use images of text only for decoration
- ❑ Text contrast is 7:1 for standard, 4.5:1 for large text
- ❑ Text blocks are no more than 80 characters wide
- ❑ Text does not appear in columns
- ❑ Text is primarily left aligned
- ❑ Paragraph spacing is at least 1.5 times line spacing

- ❑ Text can be resized without requiring scrolling
- ❑ Learner can select foreground and background colors
- ❑ Avoid using formatting to emphasize text

Readability

What Do I Do?

Minimum

Identify the language used in the document so that assistive technology can read, display, and pronounce the language correctly.

WCAG 2.2 - 3.1.1 Language of Page

All pages should have descriptive titles that make the topic or purpose of the page clear.

WCAG 2.2 - 2.4.2 Page Titled

Use headings and labels to provide clarity around how content is related.

WCAG 2.2 - 1.3.1 Info and Relationships
WCAG 3.0 - 2.7.4 Structure

It should be clear where links will take the learner next, either from the link text itself or the context in the sentence leading up to the link.

WCAG 2.2 - 2.4.4 Link Purpose (In Context)

Make sure the visual presentation of the content matches what's read out by a screen reader by sequencing information correctly.

WCAG 2.2 - 1.3.2 Meaningful Sequence

Recommended

Use headings and labels that describe the topic or purpose of the section or page.

WCAG 2.2 - 2.4.6 Headings and Labels
WCAG 3.0 – 2.7.4 Structure

Identify the language used in each passage or phrase so that assistive technology can read, display, and pronounce the language correctly. Some exceptions include proper names and technical terms.

WCAG 2.2 – 3.1.2 Language of Parts

Consider your word usage:

- Write in the active voice instead of passive voice.
- Choose short, simple words that are common and easy to understand.
- Use contractions as appropriate.
- Omit unnecessary words.

Federal Plain Language Guidelines
ISO 24495-1:2023 Plain Language

Consider your sentence structure:

- Avoid run-on sentences. Use clear, short sentences and paragraphs.
- Avoid double negatives.
- Place main ideas before exceptions and conditions.
- Use transition words between paragraphs.
- Write short paragraphs with one main idea each.

Federal Plain Language Guidelines
ISO 24495-1:2023 Plain Language

Use aids to clarify meaning, such as diagrams, tables, and illustrations.

Federal Plain Language Guidelines
ISO 24495-1:2023 Plain Language

Use parentheses sparingly and try to reword your sentences to avoid using them. These are generally not read by screen readers and may create unintended sentence structures when omitted.

EAPM Style & Accessibility Guide

Advanced

Use section headings to further organize content.

WCAG 2.2 - 2.4.10 Section Headings
WCAG 3.0 - 2.7.4 Structure

The purpose of links is clear from the link text alone. Avoid using phrases like "Read More" or "Click Here."

WCAG 2.2 - 2.4.9 Link Purpose (Link Only)
EAPM Style & Accessibility Guide
Accessible Social

Text should be readable at the 9th grade level after removing proper names and titles, or an alternate version of the text should be available that meets this recommendation. Consider Plain English and Easy English formats.

WCAG 2.2 - 3.1.5 Reading Level
Centre for Inclusive Design
Easy Read Australia
ISO 24495-1:2023 Plain Language
Accessible Social

A glossary or other mechanism exists to define unusual words, expand abbreviations, and assist with pronunciation if needed to understand context.

WCAG 2.2 - 3.1.3 Unusual Words
WCAG 2.2 - 3.1.4 Abbreviations

WCAG 2.2 – 3.1.6 Pronunciations
WCAG 3.0 – 2.2.3 Clear Language
UDL Guideline 2.1: Clarify vocabulary, symbols, and language structures
UDL Guideline 6.3: Organize information and resources

Who Benefits?

Readability makes information easier to process and understand. Simple sentence structures and familiar terms reduce cognitive load, improving comprehension and retention. This is particularly helpful for learners with cognitive impairments or learning disabilities like dyslexia.

For learners with low vision or blindness, plain language can make text easier to interpret and navigate.

Learners with hearing impairments often rely on written communication. Plain language ensures they can access information effectively, especially when instructions, procedures, or important details are involved.

Checklist: Document Readability

Minimum

- ❑ Document language is identified
- ❑ Pages have clear, descriptive titles
- ❑ Headings and labels indicate related content
- ❑ Links clearly indicate where they go
- ❑ Content is sequenced in order for screen readers

Recommended

- ❑ Headings and labels describe topics and purpose
- ❑ Passage/phrase language(s) are identified
- ❑ Write in active voice
- ❑ Choose short, simple words
- ❑ Use contractions
- ❑ Omit unnecessary words
- ❑ Use clear, short sentences
- ❑ Avoid double negatives
- ❑ Place main ideas first, then exceptions
- ❑ Use transition words
- ❑ Have one main idea per paragraph
- ❑ Use diagrams and tables to clarify meaning
- ❑ Avoid using parentheses if possible

Advanced

- ❑ Content is further organized with section headings
- ❑ Link purpose is clear from link text alone
- ❑ Text is readable at 9th grade level (or alternate format)
- ❑ Glossary is available for definitions and pronunciation

Appendix

References
Choosing Authoring Tools and Platforms with Accessibility Features
Recommended Authoring Tools and Platforms
Accessibility Tools
Reading List
Acknowledgements
About the Author

References

WCAG & ATAG

Web Content Accessibility Guidelines (WCAG) 2.2
https://www.w3.org/TR/WCAG22/

How to Meet WCAG Quick Reference
https://www.w3.org/WAI/WCAG22/quickref/

Guidance on Applying WCAG 2 to Non-Web Information and Communications Technologies
https://www.w3.org/TR/wcag2ict-22/

Web Content Accessibility Guidelines 3.0 Working Draft
https://www.w3.org/TR/wcag-3.0/

Authoring Tool Accessibility Guidelines (ATAG) 2.0
https://www.w3.org/TR/ATAG20/

Additional Guidelines

Accessible Social (2024)
https://www.accessible-social.com/

Ako Aotearoa: The Dyslexia-Friendly Style Guide (2023)
https://ako.ac.nz/knowledge-centre/dyslexia-resources/dyslexia-friendly-style-guide

Centre for Inclusive Design: Easy English versus Plain English (2020)
https://centreforinclusivedesign.org.au/wp-content/uploads/2020/04/Easy-English-vs-Plain-English_accessible.pdf

Easy Read Australia: The Easy Read Toolbox (2025)
https://www.easyreadtoolbox.info/

Emoji Accessibility for Visually Impaired People
Tigwell, G. W., Gorman, B. M., & Menzies, R. (2020).
https://eprints.bournemouth.ac.uk/33854/1/tigwell-gorman-menzies-CHI2020.pdf

Equal Access Public Media (EAPM) Style & Accessibility Guide (2025)
https://eapmstyleguide.org/

Federal Plain Language Guidelines (2011)
https://digital.gov/guides/plain-language

Federal Toolkits (2025)
https://digital.gov/topics/accessibility
https://digital.gov/topics/social-media

ISO 24495-1:2023 - Plain Language (2023)
https://www.iso.org/standard/78907.html

Universal Design for Learning Guidelines 3.0 (2024)
https://udlguidelines.cast.org/

Choosing Authoring Tools and Platforms with Accessibility Features

Before procuring any tool for online learning content creation or distribution, it's important to consider both the accessibility of the platform itself, and how accessible the content created using the platform is for learners.

A great tool acts like a spell-checker for accessibility. When evaluating a tool, look for these specific features:

- **Real-time Accessibility Checkers**: Does the tool flag a lack of color contrast or missing headers while you are typing?
- **Guided Correction**: Instead of just saying "Error," does the tool explain how to fix it?
- **Defaulting to Accessible**: When you insert a video, does the tool automatically create a placeholder for a transcript or captions?

The best tools don't treat accessibility as a "final scan." They integrate it into the creative workflow so that "done" also means "accessible."

VPATs & ACRs

A VPAT, or Voluntary Product Accessibility Template, is a self-assessment tool used by software vendors to show how their product conforms to various accessibility standards.

An ACR, or Accessibility Conformance Report, is the result of using the VPAT and should be recent, detailed, and acknowledging any known gaps. No complex software is perfectly accessible, so beware of “perfect” scores.

Recommended Authoring Tools and Platforms

LMS Accessibility

This page briefly introduces the ATAG (Authoring Tool Accessibility Guidelines) standard to help make your learning management system (LMS) and other education tools accessible to people with disabilities: https://www.w3.org/WAI/standards-guidelines/atag/education/

eLearning Content Creation

Articulate Storyline 360 offers the most granular control, including a sophisticated accessibility checker that now uses AI to suggest alt-text and help manage complex "Tab Order" for screen readers. **Rise 360** is the "accessible by default" choice, ideal for mobile-responsive content, though it is less flexible. Creators should note that while it handles text and images beautifully, certain interactive blocks still require alternative versions to be fully accessible. https://www.articulate.com/about/accessibility/

Live Training & Audience Participation

Zoom remains an industry leader in synchronous accessibility, offering robust support for screen readers, customizable keyboard shortcuts, and multi-spotlight features to keep sign language interpreters visible. Their 2026 updates have integrated "AI Companion" features that provide real-time automated captions and meeting summaries, though authors should still prioritize human-generated captions for high-stakes or legally mandated accommodations. https://zoom.com/en/accessibility/

Mentimeter stands out for its proactive approach, featuring a built-in "Accessibility Check" that audits presentations for color contrast and missing alt-text before they go live. **Poll Everywhere** provides a deeply detailed Accessibility Remediation Plan for 2026, but authors must be wary of specific interactive types which still present significant barriers for screen reader users compared to their more accessible multiple-choice options.

https://www.mentimeter.com/accessibility
https://www.polleverywhere.com/accessibility

Accessible Documents

Venngage has carved a niche as a top-tier accessible design tool by integrating an AI-powered accessibility checker that automatically tags PDF structures for headers, tables, and lists. Their platform includes a "Visual Simulator" that allows authors to view their designs through the lens of various vision impairments (like color blindness), ensuring that infographics are perceivable by all before they are published. https://venngage.com/features/accessible

A Note on Overlays

You may be familiar with accessibility overlays, or small code widgets you can add to a platform or website that promise various accessibility features. Most accessibility professionals strongly caution against using overlays, for many reasons. https://overlayfactsheet.com

Signed by over 1000 accessibility professionals.
Check out #983!

Accessibility Tools

Automated & Online Tools

WebAIM Color Contrast Checker
https://webaim.org/resources/contrastchecker

WAVE Web Accessibility Checker
https://wave.webaim.org/

A11y Project Checklist
https://www.a11yproject.com/checklist/

Readability

Flesch-Kincaid Calculator
https://flesch-kincaid-calculator.com/

Hemingway
https://hemingwayapp.com/

Readable
https://app.readable.com/text/

Inclusive Design

W3C: Accessibility, Usability, and Inclusion
https://www.w3.org/WAI/fundamentals/accessibility-usability-inclusion/

Microsoft Inclusive Design Toolkit
https://inclusive.microsoft.design/

Reading List

- [ ] Accessibility for Everyone *by Laura Kalbag*
- [ ] Demystifying Disability: What to Know, What to Say, and How to Be an Ally *by Emily Ladau*
- [ ] Design for All Learners: Create Accessible and Inclusive Learning Experiences *edited by Sarah Mercier*
- [ ] Designing Accessible Learning Content: A Practical Guide to Applying Best-Practice Accessibility Standards to L&D Resources, Second Edition *by Susi Miller*
- [ ] Inclusive Design for a Digital World: Designing with Accessibility in Mind, Second Edition *by Reginé M. Gilbert*

Accessibility Book Club

A club for passionate professionals who unite to share insights and resources on accessibility, inclusive design, and development. Visit https://www.a11ybookclub.com.

More Resources

Britne's constantly updated list of accessibility training, books, handouts, and other resources! Scan the QR code below or visit https://linktr.ee/inclusivepixel.

Acknowledgements

To Stacy - you are a constant source of inspiration, knowledge, and laughter. Thank you for inviting me to join your journey at Equal Access Public Media.

To my professional community - ATD Arizona, NSA Las Vegas, L&D Shakers, 2Gether International, and many colleagues past and present (with a few I will name personally: Jeff, Jesse, Steve, Cindy, Jen) - thank you for providing your support and guidance. Having so many places I can turn to for strategy, questions, and practical advice and applications has truly enriched my career.

To all those who couldn't see how far we've come - my mom Annie, my husband's parents, my Grandpa Meyer, my friend Robert, and many more - I wish you were still with us. I carry your lessons with me always.

And finally, to my emotional support rescue cat Brandy. (She's a fine girl.) She really likes sleeping on my laptop, and any typos are her fault. But she helped.

About the Author

Hi, I'm Britne!

I started writing the checklists that grew into this book back in 2021, when I wanted quick, simple references for myself while I was working as a freelance instructional designer. Since then, I've expanded my work into accessibility consulting and more, but I wanted to help other learning and development practitioners who have found themselves in the same place I was once in.

I've had disabilities most of my life, but I first started practicing accessibility over 20 years ago, when I learned of its importance while working as a web designer and developer. I still strive to improve my skills and deepen my knowledge through constant professional development, and I'm thrilled that you've picked up this book as part of your own accessibility journey.

I'd love for you to get in touch and tell me how you're making your own workplace more accessible. You can find me on social media (use the hashtag **#A11yBook**) or you can email me at Britne@A11yBook.com

www.ingramcontent.com/pod-product-compliance
Lightning Source LLC
LaVergne TN
LVHW010840120826
845149LV00017B/3323

* 9 7 9 8 9 8 9 6 8 1 7 2 3 *